FAVORITE RECIPES

Coca-Cola

CONTENTS

CHERRY PORK MEDALLIONS WITH COCA-COLA® 4

TERIYAKI CHICKEN 6

SPICY BBQ PARTY FRANKS 8

CROSTINI WITH EGGPLANT TAPENADE 10

COCA-COLA® GLAZED BACON-WRAPPED DATES 12

CAPRESE BRUSCHETTA 14

GAZPACHO WITH COCA-COLA® REDUCTION 16

BAYOU JAMBALAYA 18

BARBECUED RIBS WITH THICK COKE® SAUCE 20

FRUITED PORK CHOPS 22

SWEET SOUTHERN BARBECUE CHICKEN 24

ALOHA BURGERS WITH PINEAPPLE CHUTNEY 26

CHOCOLATE COCA-COLA® CAKE WITH
CHOCOLATE CREAM CHEESE FROSTING 28

CHERRY AND COKE® APPLE RINGS 30

CHERRY PORK MEDALLIONS WITH COCA-COLA®

MAKES 4 SERVINGS

1 pound pork tenderloin

1 tablespoon olive oil

1 jar (10 ounces) cherry preserves

¼ cup *Coca-Cola®*

2 tablespoons light corn syrup

¼ teaspoon ground cinnamon

¼ teaspoon ground nutmeg

¼ teaspoon ground cloves

¼ teaspoon salt

Slice tenderloin into ½-inch-thick medallions. Heat oil in large nonstick skillet over medium heat; add pork and cook about 2 minutes each side. Remove pork from skillet; set aside.

Combine cherry preserves, *Coca-Cola*, corn syrup, cinnamon, nutmeg, cloves and salt in same skillet. Bring to a boil over medium-high heat, stirring constantly, about 3 minutes.

Return pork to skillet; cover and simmer 8 to 10 minutes or until pork is cooked through.

NOTE: This recipe uses pork tenderloin with a sweet, savory sauce—perfect for a quick weeknight dish or as an easy weekend meal.

TERIYAKI CHICKEN

MAKES 4 TO 6 SERVINGS

1 pound skinless boneless chicken breasts, cut into strips

MARINADE

1 cup soy sauce

½ cup *Coca-Cola*®

2 tablespoons orange juice

1 tablespoon fresh ginger, minced

1 clove garlic, minced

Salt, black pepper and chili powder to taste

¼ cup vegetable oil

Combine all marinade ingredients and marinate chicken overnight.

Place chicken on well-oiled pan and bake at 350°F for about 30 minutes. Remove from oven, slide chicken around in pan to sop up caramelized sauce, baste with additional marinade and return to oven for another 15 minutes.

TIP: If you have any chicken left over, simply combine it with mixed greens, sliced bell peppers, green onion and cucumber for a delicious and healthful teriyaki chicken salad.

SPICY BBQ PARTY FRANKS

MAKES 6 TO 8 SERVINGS

1 tablespoon butter

1 package (1 pound) cocktail franks

⅓ cup *Coca-Cola*®

⅓ cup ketchup

2 tablespoons hot pepper sauce

1 tablespoon cider vinegar

2 tablespoons packed dark brown sugar

Heat butter in medium skillet over medium heat. Pierce cocktail franks with fork. Add franks to skillet and brown slightly.

Pour in *Coca-Cola*, ketchup, hot pepper sauce and vinegar. Stir in brown sugar; reduce heat.

Cook until sticky glaze is achieved. Serve with toothpicks.

CROSTINI WITH EGGPLANT TAPENADE

MAKES 8 SERVINGS

3 tablespoons olive oil

2 cups diced eggplant

⅓ cup diced shallots or onion

1 cup pitted kalamata olives, chopped

1 tablespoon capers with juice

½ cup red peppadew peppers, chopped with 2 tablespoons juice*

1 tablespoon balsamic vinegar

½ cup *Coca-Cola*®

½ teaspoon red pepper flakes

Salt and black pepper

Toasted baguette slices

If unavailable, may substitute with roasted red peppers.

Heat oil in large nonstick skillet over medium-high heat. Add eggplant and shallots; cook about 6 minutes or until richly golden, stirring often. Add olives, capers and peppadew peppers with their juices; continue stirring about 5 minutes or until most liquid has evaporated.

When mixture has reduced, add vinegar and *Coca-Cola*. Sprinkle with red pepper flakes, salt and black pepper.

Reduce heat to low. Cook about 15 minutes or until thickened. Stir several times during final cooking stage. Serve warm or cold on toasted baguette slices.

TIP: This versatile eggplant tapenade can also be served on top of crackers or with raw crudités.

COCA-COLA® GLAZED BACON-WRAPPED DATES

MAKES 8 SERVINGS (2 EACH)

8 slices bacon

2 tablespoons balsamic vinegar

⅓ cup *Coca-Cola®*

1 teaspoon Dijon mustard

⅛ teaspoon garlic powder

16 large dates

8 teaspoons cream cheese, divided

16 raw almonds, roasted or smoked

½ teaspoon salt

½ teaspoon black pepper

1 tablespoon unsalted butter

Preheat oven to 400°F. Cut bacon slices in half and cook in medium skillet over medium heat 1 minute on each side. Drain on paper towel and set aside. (Bacon should be soft.) Discard bacon grease.

Add vinegar, *Coca-Cola*, mustard and garlic powder to skillet. Cook on medium heat 3 to 4 minutes or until mixture becomes a thickened glaze.

While glaze is cooking, slice one side of each date lengthwise and remove pit. Fill each date with ½ teaspoon cream cheese and 1 almond, then pinch date closed.

Wrap each stuffed date with ½ slice bacon and secure with wooden toothpicks. Remove glaze from heat and stir in salt, pepper and butter. In two nonstick rimmed baking sheets, drizzle 1 tablespoon sauce and place 8 dates side by side in each.

Evenly drizzle remaining sauce over the tops and bake 10 minutes. Remove from oven and let cool slightly, 5 minutes.

CAPRESE BRUSCHETTA

MAKES 12 SERVINGS

¼ cup balsamic vinegar

2 tablespoons Coca-Cola®

Garlic powder, divided

6 plum tomatoes, seeded and diced

12 large fresh basil leaves, chopped

¼ cup extra virgin olive oil emulsified* with 1 tablespoon Coca-Cola®

1 teaspoon salt

Black pepper

¼ cup (½ stick) softened butter

1 French baguette, cut into 24 slices

12 small balls fresh mozzarella cheese, cut in half**

Fresh basil leaves

*To emulsify means to blend two or more unblendable substances such as vinegar and oil. This can easily be done with a whisk, hand blender or food processor.

**If unavailable, may use an 8-ounce fresh mozzarella ball. Cut ball in quarters and slice each quarter into 6 slices, making 24 slices total.

Bring vinegar, *Coca-Cola* and pinch of garlic powder to a boil over medium-high heat in small saucepan. Reduce heat to medium-low and cook about 10 to 15 minutes or until mixture is reduced to a syrup. Remove mixture from heat to cool.

Meanwhile, lightly toss tomatoes with chopped basil in medium bowl. Stir in emulsified oil/*Coca-Cola* and season with salt and pepper.

Microwave butter in small microwave-safe dish 15 to 20 seconds. Spread baguette slices with butter and sprinkle lightly with garlic powder. Toast baguette slices on baking sheet under broiler about 1 minute on each side or until crisp. To serve, top bread slices with 1 heaping tablespoon of tomato/basil mixture and 2 cheese halves. Drizzle with cooled syrup and garnish with basil leaves.

GAZPACHO WITH COCA-COLA® REDUCTION

MAKES 4 TO 6 SERVINGS

⅔ cup *Coca-Cola*®, divided

½ cup balsamic vinegar, divided

¼ cup olive oil

⅔ cup tomato or vegetable juice

⅛ teaspoon ground red pepper

3 tomatoes, chopped

1 red bell pepper, chopped

1 medium sweet onion

1 large shallot, chopped

1 large cucumber, seeded and chopped

Salt and black pepper

½ cup sour cream or plain yogurt

½ cup fresh basil leaves

Bring half of *Coca-Cola* and half of vinegar to a boil over medium-high heat in medium saucepan. Cook about 3 minutes or until liquid measures about 2 tablespoons.

Meanwhile, whisk together remaining *Coca-Cola*, remaining vinegar, oil, tomato juice and ground red pepper in small bowl. Pulse tomatoes, bell pepper, onion, shallot, cucumber and tomato juice mixture together in food processor or blender until mixture becomes a rough purée. (Work in batches, if necessary.)

Season with salt and black pepper and chill several hours. Serve gazpacho in chilled bowls with dollop of sour cream. Drizzle with cooled syrup and garnish with basil.

BAYOU JAMBALAYA

MAKES 8 SERVINGS

2 large stalks celery, diced

1 onion, diced

28 ounces smoked sausage, cut into ¼-inch slices

3 cloves garlic, chopped

1 red bell pepper, diced

1 tablespoon chopped fresh parsley

1 teaspoon dried oregano

1 teaspoon dried thyme

½ teaspoon paprika

½ cup *Coca-Cola*®

½ cup dry white wine

1 can (about 14 ounces) diced tomatoes, undrained

3 cups water

1 pound uncooked medium shrimp, peeled and deveined

1 bay leaf

1½ cups uncooked long-grain rice

Combine celery, onion and sausage in large skillet over medium-high heat and cook 5 minutes. Add garlic and bell pepper; stir and cook 3 to 4 minutes. Add parsley, oregano, thyme and paprika; stir and cook 1 minute.

Add *Coca-Cola*, wine, tomatoes, water, shrimp, bay leaf and rice. Increase to high heat, bring to a boil, then reduce and simmer, covered, 25 minutes or until rice is tender. Remove and discard bay leaf.

TIP: You can make jambalaya with beef, pork, chicken, duck, shrimp, oysters, crayfish, sausage or any combination.

BARBECUED RIBS WITH THICK COKE® SAUCE

MAKES 6 SERVINGS

2 medium onions, finely chopped

¾ cup *Coca-Cola®*

¾ cup ketchup

2 tablespoons vinegar

2 tablespoons Worcestershire sauce

½ teaspoon chili powder

½ teaspoon salt

2 tablespoons olive oil

6 pounds pork baby back ribs (2 racks), halved

Combine onions, *Coca-Cola*, ketchup, vinegar, Worcestershire sauce, chili powder and salt in medium saucepan over high heat. Bring to a boil. Cover pan; reduce heat and simmer about 45 minutes or until sauce is very thick. Stir occasionally.

Preheat grill for indirect cooking over medium heat. Rub 1 tablespoon oil over each rack of ribs. Lightly coat with barbecue sauce.

Place ribs meat side down on grid sprayed with nonstick cooking spray. Grill 30 minutes or until ribs are tender, turning and basting with sauce occasionally.

Bring remaining sauce to a boil in small saucepan over medium-high heat; boil 1 minute. Serve ribs with sauce.

FRUITED PORK CHOPS

MAKES 4 SERVINGS

4 rib, loin or shoulder pork chops or smoked pork chops, ½- to ¾-inch thick

1 teaspoon salt

⅛ teaspoon black pepper

⅛ teaspoon ground ginger

1 medium apple

1 medium lemon or orange

2 tablespoons packed brown sugar

½ cup *Coca-Cola*®

1 tablespoon cornstarch

Trim fat from chops, then brown them on each side in ungreased skillet. Lay chops in shallow baking pan. Do not overlap. Sprinkle with salt, pepper and ginger.

Core unpeeled apple, cut crosswise into 4 thick slices. Cut lemon into 4 slices; remove seeds. Lay lemon slices atop apple slices and place on each chop.

Sprinkle with brown sugar. Pour *Coca-Cola* around chops. Cover tightly. Bake in 350°F oven for 45 minutes.

Blend cornstarch with 2 tablespoons water until smooth. Stir into meat juices. Bake, uncovered, 15 minutes longer or until meat is fork-tender. Spoon sauce over fruit chops to glaze.

SWEET SOUTHERN BARBECUE CHICKEN

MAKES 4 SERVINGS

2 to 3 tablespoons olive oil, divided

½ cup chopped onion

1 clove garlic, minced

½ cup packed brown sugar

1 teaspoon dry mustard

1 tablespoon honey mustard

1 tablespoon Dijon mustard

1 cup *Coca-Cola*®

2 tablespoons balsamic vinegar

2 tablespoons cider vinegar

2 tablespoons Worcestershire sauce

½ cup ketchup

2 to 3 pounds boneless skinless chicken thighs

SAUCE

Heat 1 tablespoon oil in medium skillet over medium heat. Add onion and garlic and cook 2 minutes.

Add next 4 ingredients; bring to a boil over medium-high heat, reduce heat and simmer, uncovered, 20 minutes or until sauce thickens.

Add *Coca-Cola*, balsamic vinegar, cider vinegar, Worcestershire sauce and ketchup; stir.

Simmer 15 to 20 minutes, until sauce thickens. Remove from heat.

CHICKEN

Heat remaining oil in large skillet over medium-high heat. Add half of chicken and cook about 5 to 7 minutes per side or until cooked through. After turning, brush chicken with barbecue sauce. Brush both sides again with sauce in the last 1 to 2 minutes of cooking. Serve chicken with additional sauce. Repeat with remaining chicken.

ALOHA BURGERS WITH PINEAPPLE CHUTNEY

MAKES 6 SERVINGS

2 tablespoons butter

2 tablespoons packed dark brown sugar

¼ cup *Coca-Cola*®

¼ cup balsamic vinegar

½ medium red onion, diced

1 small tomato, seeded and diced

1½ cups diced pineapple

2 pounds ground beef

2 tablespoons teriyaki sauce

2 teaspoons Worcestershire sauce

2 teaspoons onion powder

1½ teaspoons salt

2 teaspoons black pepper

Additional salt and black pepper

6 brioche buns,* toasted

If unavailable, substitute hamburger buns.

Melt butter in medium saucepan over medium-low heat; stir in brown sugar until blended. Stir in **Coca-Cola** and vinegar; bring to a boil. Reduce heat to low; simmer 20 minutes, stirring frequently.

Stir in onion; cook and stir 2 minutes over medium heat. Add tomato and pineapple, stir to coat and turn off heat.

Combine beef, teriyaki sauce, Worcestershire sauce, onion powder, 1½ teaspoons salt and 2 teaspoons pepper in medium bowl; mix lightly. Shape into 6 patties.

Cook burgers under broiler or on grill pan over medium-high heat, 6 minutes on each side. When cooked to desired doneness, keep warm. Return pineapple mixture to high heat and cook 1 minute. Season with additional salt and pepper. Top each burger with a heaping spoonful of pineapple mixture. Serve on toasted brioche buns.

CHOCOLATE COCA-COLA® CAKE WITH CHOCOLATE CREAM CHEESE FROSTING

MAKES 1 CAKE

1 box (18¼ ounces) chocolate cake mix

1 cup *Coca-Cola®*

¼ cup water

½ cup vegetable oil

3 eggs

Chocolate Cream Cheese Frosting (recipe follows)

CHOCOLATE CREAM CHEESE FROSTING

4 cups powdered sugar, sifted

⅓ cup unsweetened cocoa powder

1 package (8 ounces) cream cheese, softened

½ cup (1 stick) butter, softened

1 teaspoon vanilla

Preheat oven to 350°F. Grease 2 (8-inch) round cake pans; set aside.

Combine cake mix, ***Coca-Cola***, water, oil and eggs in large bowl. Beat at low speed of electric mixer until blended; beat at medium speed 2 minutes. Divide batter between prepared pans.

Bake 30 to 35 minutes or until toothpick inserted into center of cakes comes out clean. Cool in pans on wire racks 10 minutes. Remove from pans to wire racks; cool completely.

Meanwhile, prepare Chocolate Cream Cheese Frosting. Combine sifted powdered sugar and cocoa in large bowl; set aside.

Beat cream cheese, butter and vanilla extract in large bowl until smooth. Gradually fold in powdered sugar and cocoa.

Place 1 cake layer on serving plate and frost top and sides with Chocolate Cream Cheese Frosting. Repeat with second layer.

CHERRY AND COKE® APPLE RINGS

MAKES 4 SERVINGS

3 Granny Smith or other tart apples, peeled and cored

½ teaspoon plus ¼ teaspoon sugar-free, cherry-flavored gelatin powder

⅓ cup *Coca-Cola*®

⅓ cup nondairy whipped topping

Slice apples crosswise into ¼-inch-thick rings; remove seeds. Place stacks of apple rings in large microwavable bowl; sprinkle with gelatin. Pour **Coca-Cola** over rings.

Cover loosely with waxed paper. Microwave on HIGH (100%) 5 minutes or until liquid is boiling. Allow to stand, covered, 5 minutes. Arrange on dessert plates. Serve warm with whipped topping.